Carving the Female Face

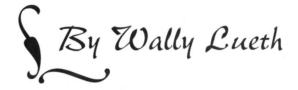 By Wally Lueth

Fox
Chapel Publishing Co. Inc.

1970 Broad Street • East Petersburg, PA 17520 • www.carvingworld.com

Publisher: Alan Giagnocavo
Project Editor: Ayleen Stellhorn
Desktop Specialist: Linda L. Eberly, Eberly Designs Inc.

ISBN # 1–56523–145-7

Library of Congress Catalog Card Number 90–91859

To order your copy of this book,
please send check or money order
for $12.95 plus $3.00 shipping to:
Fox Chapel Publishing
Book Orders
1970 Broad Street
East Petersburg, PA 17520

Or visit us on the web at
www.carvingworld.com

Manufactured in the USA

Table of Contents

About the Author

Walter Henry Lueth is known by his friends as Wally or Walt. He carves under the name "W. Henry Lüth." The umlaut above the "u" indicates his German heritage.

Wally began his career in wood as a young apprentice in the furniture and fixture business. After achieving his goals along those lines, he retired and began carving.

The methods in this book are the results of Wally's studies with such expert carvers as Harold Enlow, and artists such as Maurice Harvey, Giles Jacques Cloutier and Daniel Beauchand, all of St. Jean Port Joli, Quebec. Further studies under Benn Bunyar, nationally known stone sculptor of Independence, Missouri, enhanced Wally's skill for carving faces.

After teaching these skills to others for several years, Wally began to get inquiries about writing a book. Wally self-published the first edition of *How to Carve Pretty Faces* in 1990. This new, revised edition includes additional photographs and drawings.

Foreword

The world of carving always welcomes a new book, especially one that is helpful on a difficult subject. Carving pretty women's faces is just such a subject, and my friend Wally has come up with a solution in this volume. Wally will take you through step by step to complete a pretty face which will make life–and carving–a little easier for you. So, say goodbye to all of those carvings that look like men with dresses on, and welcome the "Ohs!" and "Ahs!" of friends and customers when they see what you can do after a little practice using the methods explained in *Carving the Female Face*.

Harold Enlow

Introduction

The intention of writing *Pretty Faces* is to share with you a method of carving pretty feminine faces either of your own design or by using the patterns provided within this publication.

Some of the problems we as carvers face are as follows:

- flat faces (flat eyes, flat lips, flat eyeballs);
- not knowing proper proportions and locations of the features of the face;
- lack of practice;
- not knowing exactly what we want when we begin a project;
- after deciding what we want, not knowing how to get there;
- tools that are not sharp enough:
- not knowing which tool to use;
- not knowing the sequence to follow;
- not being able to choose good wood;
- and not knowing how to begin.

It is my contention that one of the most important tools an artist uses is a pencil. Be willing to pick up a pencil and draw out your plans. Be willing to pick up a pencil and draw or sketch your lines on the piece you are carving. The pencil helps assure that you make the cuts exactly where you want them and that the cuts are not made haphazardly, thereby "occasionally" producing what you want. The pencil might be considered to be the most important tool of the artist simply because it can help produce consistent results.

Although the pencil may be the tool that should be most used by the artist/carver, practice will be the element that improves results over all else. Picking up a tool occasionally does not a good carver make. Practice! Practice! Practice! Remember the old adage you heard in school that said something like: "If at first…?" That refers to practice. Without practice, consistent results are almost impossible to achieve.

Because third dimension perception is sometimes difficult to achieve, and some of us have difficulty moving directly from a "flat" design on paper to a round finished product, I have found a clay model to be a good starting point; therefore, the first chapter begins with clay.

Remember the three main elements to successfully carving a "pretty face" are use a pencil, sharpen your tools, and practice, practice, practice.

Chapter One

Getting Started

PROCEDURE

The general procedures to follow in introducing carvers to carving pretty faces are as follows:

1. Decide what you, the carver; want your final piece to look like.
2. Choose a pattern from this book or draw your own design.
3. Decide what size you want your final piece to be. I have found a 4-in. head size to yield a piece approximately 9-in. high when finished.
4. Choose your wood. Basswood is best for flesh color.
5. Make a clay model.
6. Prepare "story boards" of facial features.
7. Practice each feature.
8. Carve a model of the face.
9. Prepare for your final piece.
10. Carve your final piece.
11. Finish your work of art and mount it for display.

TIPS FOR SUCCESS

As we have heard from our teachers throughout our lifetimes, practice makes perfect; do not expect to hear anything different here. Practice! Practice! Practice!

Sharp tools are an absolute necessity for the precision cutting you will use in carving a pretty face.

Remember to have a pencil with you at all times; be willing to use it frequently

HELPFUL HINTS

One thing that helps is to work under incandescent or natural lighting; fluorescent will not give you the shadows you need for even features. I find that a gooseneck lamp strategically placed for even lighting works well. Uneven lighting or fluorescent lighting seems to defeat efforts to match the features from one side to the other.

- The more detail you complete, the more shadows you cast, the more pleasing effects you achieve.
- The clay model was done with no hair. Placing plastic wrap on the scalp before adding clay for the hair allows me to remove the hair and easily change hairstyles.
- Remove all grit from sanding before using your tools. The grit will dull your tools.
- Keep your tools extremely sharp. Dull tools crush fiber and tear the wood. They also cause you to apply too much pressure and lose control of your cuts.
- Practice each feature just prior to attempting it on your model or final piece. Practice will do a tremendous amount in enhancing your results.
- The pencil is your primary tool. If you do not know where you are going, how can you get there? Measure and re-measure. The placement and proportions of the facial features are all-important in carving a pretty face.
- Constructive criticism from friends can make you look at your piece from different perspectives. Ask for and listen to constructive criticism. If you find yourself making excuses for the way things are going, back off and criticize yourself.
- As you work, frequently back off and look at what you have done. Artists who apply wet, gooey substances to canvas say that the rule of thumb is to paint for five minutes, then back off and view for five minutes.
- A motorized muslin wheel close to your work area encourages frequent buffing, whereas one in your garage or elsewhere does not lend itself to having sharp tools.
- If you find a defect in the wood, try to either work around it or work with it.
- Work from one side of your piece to the other; whatever you do to one side of the facial features, immediately do the same to the other side.
- Give your piece an appropriate mount. I like to cut walnut into an oval and router around the edges. The oval shape seems to flow with the feminine curves.
- For a finish that enriches the wood and leaves it

white, I use clear bowling alley wax by either H. F. Staples & Company, Inc. of Merrimack, New Hampshire or by The Butcher Polish Co., Boston Massachusetts. If you have a difficult time finding this type of wax, try asking at a bowling alley, or try a janitorial supply store.

- Please keep in mind that it is your eye that likes or dislikes what it sees.

LIST OF TOOLS

I use the following tools to carve a face that measures approximately 4 1/2 inches from chin to top of skull and approximately 3 inches wide.

For the roughing out:
> gouge, 20 mm, 10 sweep (deep)
> gouge, 20 to 30 mm, 4 sweep (shallow)

Outlining eyes and mouth:
> v-tool, 2 mm

Facial features and finishing tools:
> gouge, 8 mm, 7 sweep (medium)
> gouge, 12 mm, 7 sweep (medium)
> gouge, 6 mm, 5 sweep (medium)
> gouge, 6 mm, 10 sweep (deep)
> carving knife, 5/8 in. to 3/4 in. fishtail

Hair:
> no v-tools
> gouge, 12 mm, 10 sweep (deep)
> gouge, 6 mm, 10 sweep (deep)
> gouge, 2 mm, 10 sweep, (deep)

A power tool can be used for removing the material inside the nostril and from the pupils of the eye, but really is not necessary.

I use several grades of sandpaper on the hair, beginning with 100 grit, then reducing to 280 or finer for the final sanding. On the face, I use only a 200 or 300 grit. Always sand with the grain, never against it.

You may find that you have other tools that will do the job. I do not recommend that you run out and buy tools that you can get by without.

CHOOSING A PATTERN

Before you begin carving, you would be wise to establish in your own mind's eye what your final product will look like when it is finished. You may choose to design your own pattern or use one from this book; or you might find a pattern from another source.

Whatever pattern you decide on should have both a profile view and a front view; the two must fit together to form a whole. You may check this by measuring from the top of the head (the place on your pattern that would be the crest of the skull) to the chin, excluding hair or neck. The cheeks should be at the widest part of the oval shape you will be cutting out for the front view. This will be simple on the sample blocks, as these patterns have no hair.

When choosing a pattern for your finished piece, using a piece of tracing paper, place it over the front view of your pattern and draw an oval which would give you the shape of the face from chin to top of skull; make certain that the profile view and the front view match.

One thing I have found is that proportion and location of the facial features are more important than the quality of your carving. Make certain that your pattern looks the way you like it before you proceed.

Next, make a template from stiff paper, cardboard or plastic. Both profile and oval should be treated in this manner. Now you have a good basis for beginning your practice block.

CHOOSING YOUR WOOD

One of the most important parts of carving is the choice of wood. If you do not choose your wood discriminately, your efforts could end in disappointment.

I recommend firm, tight-grained basswood with a light color and few or no flaws. By flaws, I mean the visible brown spots that look somewhat like moles. If you see any of those, check the end grain of the wood for where the flaw begins and the grain of the wood for where the flaw emerges. You can work around a few flaws without fear of interference; however, try to avoid having a flaw in the facial features.

Occasionally, a piece of wood will contain one or more holes from a boring beetle. If you come across one, check all your chips for more holes. An excessive number might indicate that your work will have a hole in a strategic location.

Another flaw to look for is referred to as "spalting." This usually manifests itself by a dark area, or it may look like dark specks on your wood. Spalting is an indication of fungus penetration into the wood. A lot of spalting will indicate a weakness in the wood.

Choose your wood carefully; do not disappoint yourself with poor results because of poor wood quality. Your sharpest tools should feel resistance in a firm piece of wood.

Chapter Two

Reference

Reference material is another important aspect of carving the female face. You cannot carve a pretty face without understanding the basics of what lies beneath. The following pages include illustrations showing the muscle and bone structure of the face. (A good anatomy book will help you further your studies). I have also included several drawings that I use in my classes to explain anatomy.

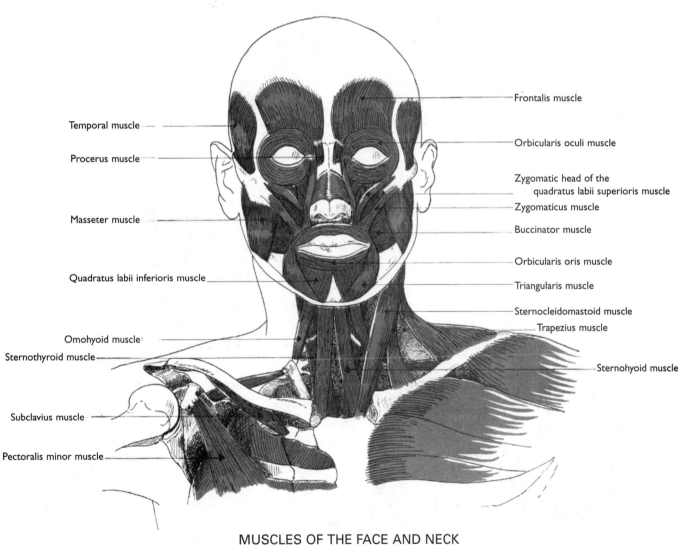

Temporal muscle —

Procerus muscle —

Masseter muscle —

Quadratus labii inferioris muscle —

Omohyoid muscle —

Sternothyroid muscle —

Subclavius muscle —

Pectoralis minor muscle —

Frontalis muscle

Orbicularis oculi muscle

Zygomatic head of the
quadratus labii superioris muscle

Zygomaticus muscle

Buccinator muscle

Orbicularis oris muscle

Triangularis muscle

Sternocleidomastoid muscle

Trapezius muscle

Sternohyoid muscle

MUSCLES OF THE FACE AND NECK

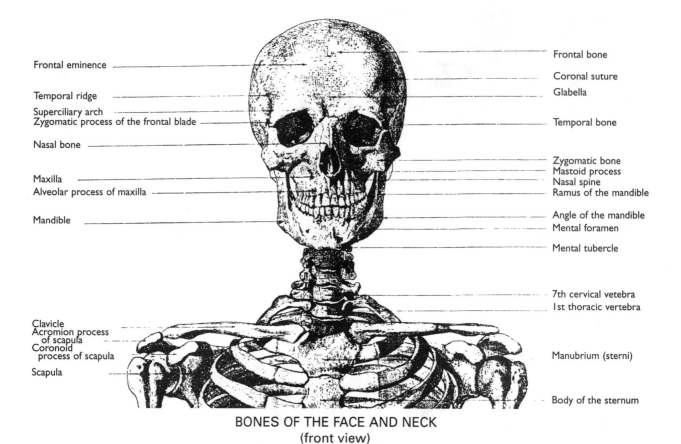

Frontal eminence

Temporal ridge

Superciliary arch
Zygomatic process of the frontal blade

Nasal bone

Maxilla
Alveolar process of maxilla

Mandible

Clavicle
Acromion process
of scapula
Coronoid
process of scapula

Scapula

Frontal bone

Coronal suture

Glabella

Temporal bone

Zygomatic bone
Mastoid process
Nasal spine
Ramus of the mandible

Angle of the mandible
Mental foramen

Mental tubercle

7th cervical vetebra
1st thoracic vertebra

Manubrium (sterni)

Body of the sternum

BONES OF THE FACE AND NECK
(front view)

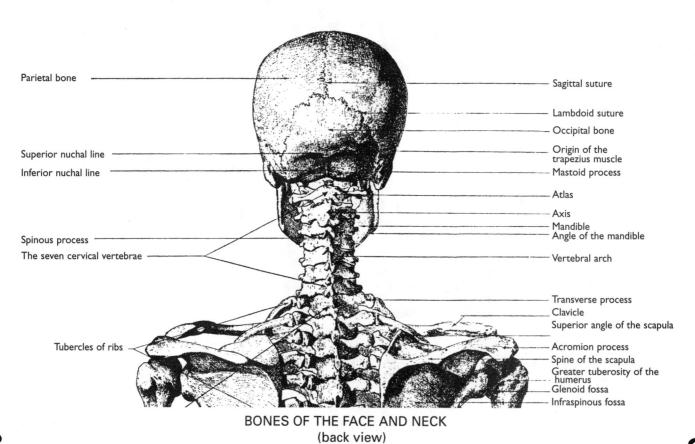

Parietal bone

Superior nuchal line

Inferior nuchal line

Spinous process

The seven cervical vertebrae

Tubercles of ribs

Sagittal suture

Lambdoid suture

Occipital bone

Origin of the
trapezius muscle

Mastoid process

Atlas

Axis
Mandible
Angle of the mandible

Vertebral arch

Transverse process
Clavicle
Superior angle of the scapula

Acromion process
Spine of the scapula
Greater tuberosity of the
humerus
Glenoid fossa
Infraspinous fossa

BONES OF THE FACE AND NECK
(back view)

Carving the Female Face

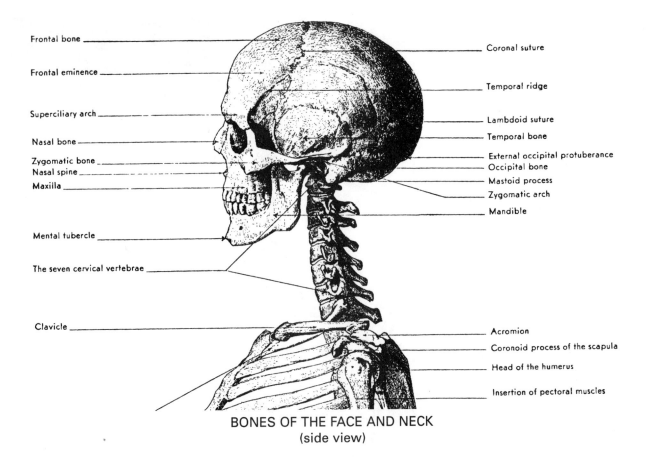

Frontal bone

Frontal eminence

Superciliary arch

Nasal bone

Zygomatic bone

Nasal spine

Maxilla

Mental tubercle

The seven cervical vertebrae

Clavicle

Coronal suture

Temporal ridge

Lambdoid suture

Temporal bone

External occipital protuberance

Occipital bone

Mastoid process

Zygomatic arch

Mandible

Acromion

Coronoid process of the scapula

Head of the humerus

Insertion of pectoral muscles

BONES OF THE FACE AND NECK
(side view)

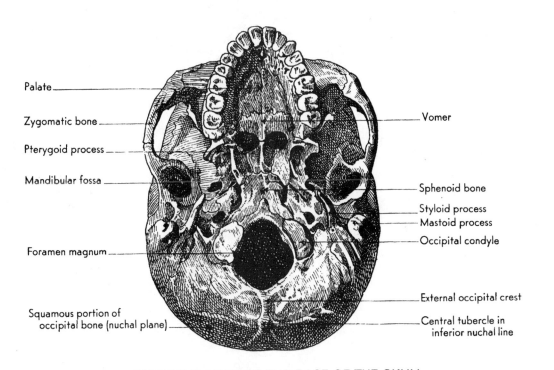

Palate

Zygomatic bone

Pterygoid process

Mandibular fossa

Foramen magnum

Squamous portion of
occipital bone (nuchal plane)

Vomer

Sphenoid bone

Styloid process

Mastoid process

Occipital condyle

External occipital crest

Central tubercle in
inferior nuchal line

EXTERNAL VIEW OF THE BASE OF THE SKULL

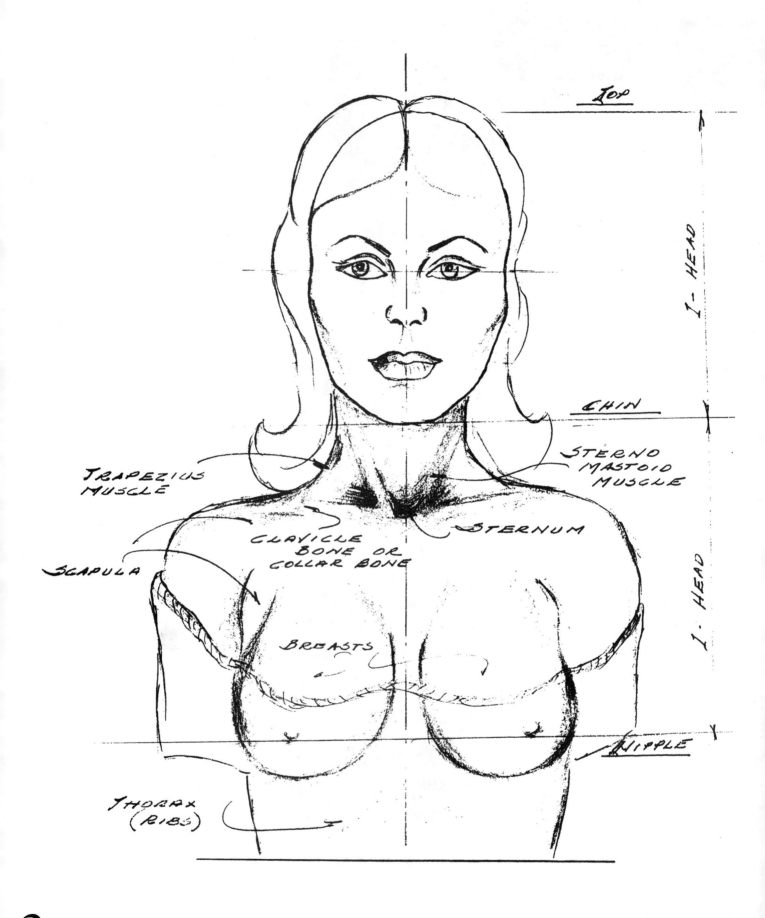

Top

I - Head

Chin

Sterno
Mastoid
Muscle

Trapezius
Muscle

Sternum

Clavicle
Bone or
Collar Bone

Scapula

I - Head

Breasts

Nipple

Thorax
(Ribs)

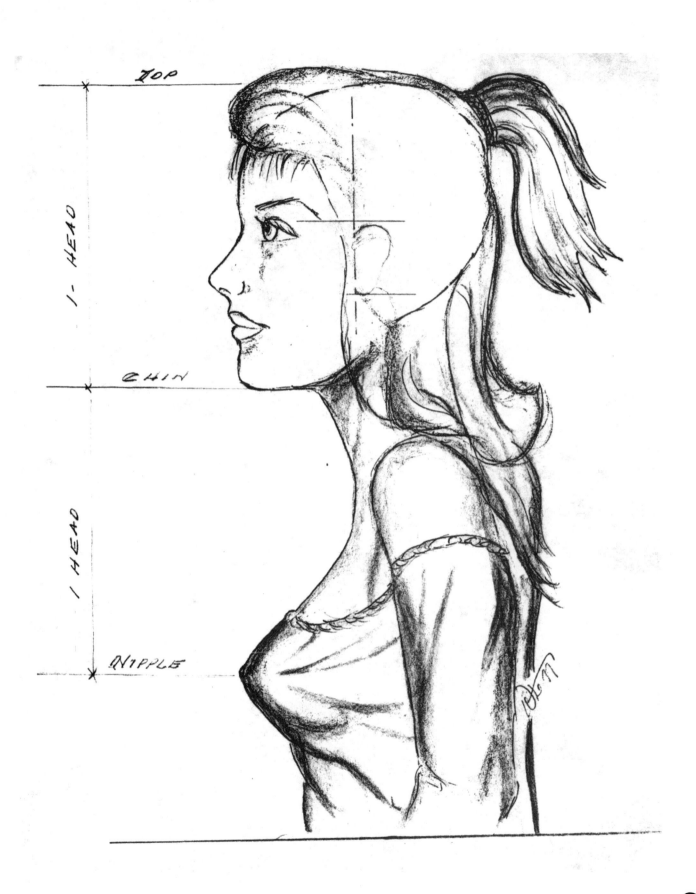

TOP

1 - HEAD

CHIN

1 HEAD

NIPPLE

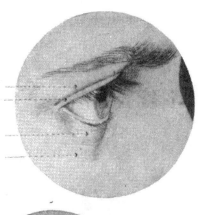

Orbital portion of
the upper eyelid

Ocular portion of
the upper eyelid

Ocular portion of
the lower eyelid

Orbital portion of
the lower eyelid

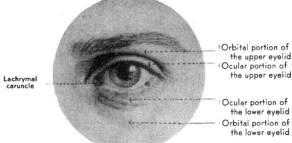

Lachrymal
caruncle

Orbital portion of
the upper eyelid

Ocular portion of
the upper eyelid

Ocular portion of
the lower eyelid

Orbital portion of
the lower eyelid

TEAR GLAND

BROW

LOW

HIGH

LID

IRIS

PUPIL

TEAR DUCT

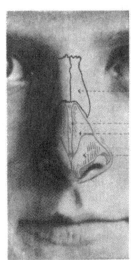

Nasal bone

} Triangular cartilage

Alar cartilage

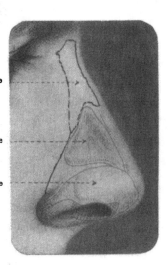

Nasal bone

Triangular cartilage

Alar cartilage

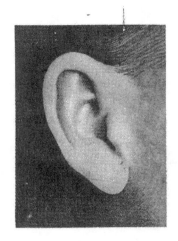

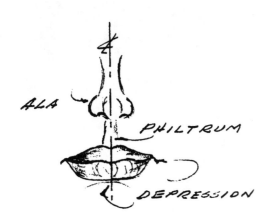

ALA

PHILTRUM

DEPRESSION

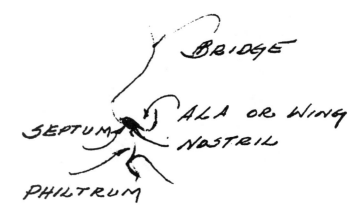

BRIDGE

SEPTUM

ALA OR WING

NOSTRIL

PHILTRUM

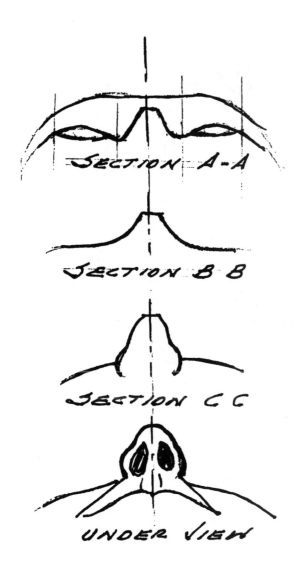

SECTION A-A

SECTION B B

SECTION C C

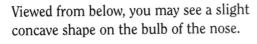

UNDER VIEW

Viewed from below, you may see a slight concave shape on the bulb of the nose.

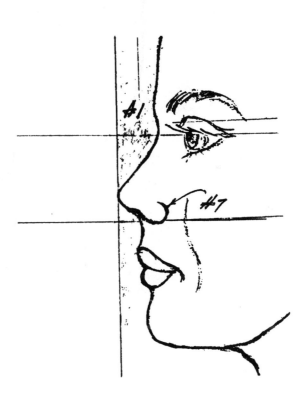

#1

#7

Viewed from the profile, you will note that the nose normally lies half in the face with the other half protruding beyond the top of the upper lip.

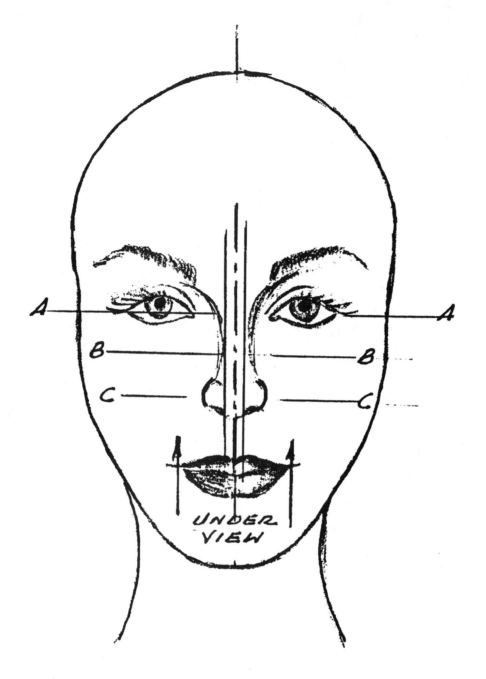

When viewed straight on from eye level, you will note that the nose angles back and up at an approximate 30 degree angle.

FEMALE

YOUNG LADY

OLD LADY

GLAMOUR GIRL

Lili St. Cyr

GLAMOUR GIRLS

"Pretty faces" can be found anywhere. These stock photographs of female models make good starting points for creating your own patterns. Keep a sketchbook of ideas. You may never use some of the faces you sketch, but others may prove to be a starting place for a great pattern.

Carving the Female Face

Carving the Female Face

Chapter Three

A Clay Model

Preparing a clay model before carving your wooden model is easy and practical.

Begin with a 2 in. by 6 in. by 6 in. block of wood and a 6 in. dowel. Measure your dowel and drill a hole approximately $1/2$ in. deep in the center of your block. Glue your dowel into the hole.

Take a piece of Styrofoam cut to a ball shape (this does not need to be accurate) or a Styrofoam ball and jam it down on the top of the dowel. This will take up some of the space inside your model's head and allow you to use less clay. It will also help hold the clay in place.

I have been using "Roma Plastilina" for our models. Clay and a few tools can be acquired at most craft shops.

It is re-useable and will not harden. It is handy for modeling other parts of the anatomy as well; for example, hands give some carvers a difficult time.

Apply your clay and work it into the basic shape of the head. Work it with your hands or tools until you achieve the proportions and appearance you want your finished product to have.

I have found that putting plastic wrap on the scalp of the clay model allows me to put hair on the model yet still have the flexibility of removing the hair and putting on a new hairstyle.

I recommend you attend a few classes in clay sculpture if they are available to you.

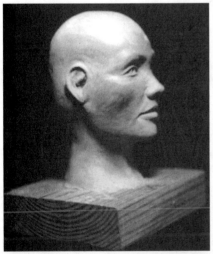

Making a clay model will help you refine the features of the finished piece. A piece of plastic wrap separates the hair from the head so the hairstyle can be removed and changed easily.

EYES

Begin with your pencil.

There are two features that basically make up the expression in a face: the eyes and the mouth. While other areas of the face contribute to expression, the eyes and the mouth establish a face's primary demeanor.

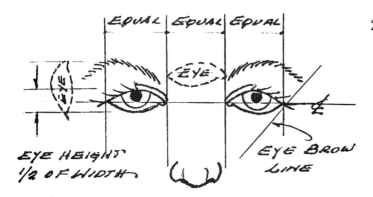

EQUAL | EQUAL | EQUAL

EYE

EYE HEIGHT 1/2 OF WIDTH

EYE BROW LINE

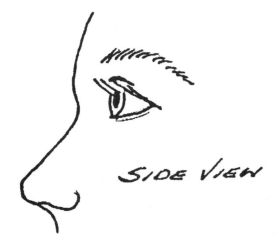

SIDE VIEW

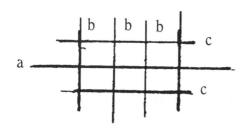

a

b | b | b

c

c

1. Draw a horizontal line (a); divide it into three parts vertically (b); divide the two outside vertical spaces into thirds. The eye should be approximately two times as wide as it is high so draw two more horizontal lines, equal distance above and below to indicate the position of the top of the eye (c). From this point, there are three basic steps to drawing an eye. Remember, the eye height is 1/2 the width.

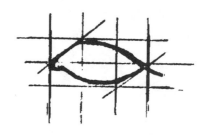

2. Draw a line on an approximate 45 degree angle from the nose/tear duct vertical line side of the eye, up approximately one third the distance to the outside vertical line. From this point, draw a long sweeping line down and barely beyond the horizontal line where the outside or temple/side vertical intersects with the horizontal line. Repeat this process only upside down and back toward the nose side, easing into a small oval for the tear duct; in other words, one third down and toward the nose side, then sweeping up.

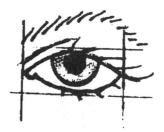

3. The iris covers approximately 50 percent of the total length of the eye. The top of the iris goes under the upper lid; the bottom of the iris shows above the lower lid. The pupil should be drawn in at the exact center of the iris. The lash and the brow line can be drawn in, if desired, at this point.

Practice drawing many times both the left and right eyes. Remember that practice, practice, practice will help you to develop your skills to an acceptable level.

Carving the Female Face

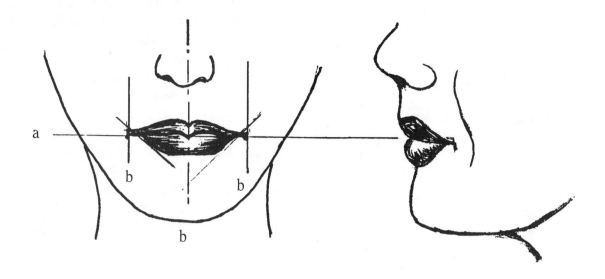

MOUTH

Begin with your pencil.

As stated on the previous page, the expression of a face is determined primarily by the eyes and the mouth. The mouth, while perhaps easier than the eyes, is equally as important.

Two simple steps will produce a drawing of the mouth. Remember that the mouth is approximately the same width as two eyes; in other words, the mouth is two eyes wide.

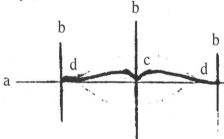

1. Draw a horizontal line (a); draw three vertical lines, approximately one eye-width apart (b). The center vertical line will be the centerline of the mouth. The horizontal line will be referred to as the mouth line. Draw a very short "v" on the vertical centerline. From the top of the "v" lines draw a very shallow cupid's bow to the intersection of the outside vertical lines and the mouth line (d). This bow represents the line where the top lip and the bottom lip meet.

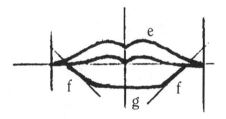

2. The next step is to repeat that bow; but, this time, draw your bow above the first bow, establishing the upper lip (e). The bottom lip should begin inside the outer vertical lines, indicating that the lower lip comes under the upper lip. The lines from the outer verticals should descend at an approximate 45 degree angle toward the center of the lip (f). Next, draw a horizontal line from between the two 45 degree lines (g). The lower lip can be rounded to these lines. The height of the lips can be determined by you, remembering that the lower lip is a farther distance from the horizontal mouth line than the upper lip. The lip looks rather nice with the approximate height of the upper lip being a little less than $1/2$ of the overall height of the lips, and the lower lip being a little more than $1/2$ of the overall height of the lips. The overall height of the lips is appealing at approximately two thirds the width of the eye.

NOSE

Begin with your pencil.

Even though the nose does not lend expression to the face, it is important to have an attractive nose, in proportion to the other features, in order to produce a pretty face.

The nose at the nostrils is approximately one eye wide. It lies half inside the face; half protrudes off the face. The nose is attractive when the tip sets in approximately perpendicular lines (90 degrees). The nose will be discussed again later in this book.

Practice drawing noses. Remember, when drawing the profile, the nose lies half in the face and half off of the face.

Study these illustrations carefully as the nature of the up and out angle can be a little confusing. Working this problem out on your clay model may save you time and trouble when you begin carving in wood.

The width of the nose is normally the same as the width of one eye; however, to make an attractive female face, we may want to under-emphasize the nose. I suggest making it slightly narrower at the bulb end and making certain that it blends into the cheek gently. Use a gouge that is shallow enough that it will not over-emphasize the nose and make it separate from the rest of the face. Note: The mouth is cone shaped, as is the nose, but it flares farther away from the centerline.

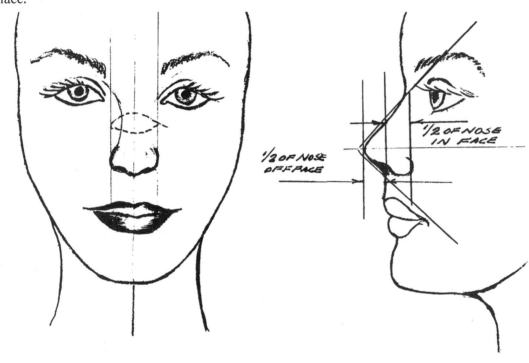

1. Draw a top-heavy "C."

2. Draw a running "U" and another "C" to indicate the rim or helix of the ear.

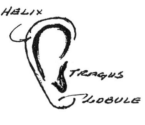

3.   Draw in the lazy "Y."

EARS

Begin with your pencil.

Even though most sculptors cover the ears with hair or hats, I feel that it is important for you to realize the location of the ear, as well as how to draw and carve it, so that you may have ears, or at least part of an ear, if you desire. Occasionally one ear is fully exposed while the other is partially exposed, or covered completely.

The ear lies from the upper lid of the eye to the lower part of the nose and back on the head behind the centerline. (Refer to sketch)

The ear may be drawn in a few easy steps using the alphabet.

Carving the Female Face

FACE AND HEAD

Begin with your pencil.

In order for a carver to accomplish a nicely finished face, head or figure, it is necessary to know what is underneath. Basically the front view of a pretty face is oval or egg shaped with a slight flattening at the temple area. The profile should reflect the skull, including the jaw line and brain cavity, and reflect the nose as protruding approximately half beyond the upper lip, and half back into the face.

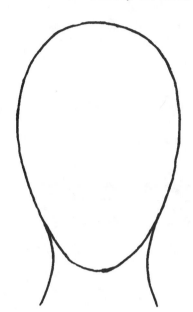

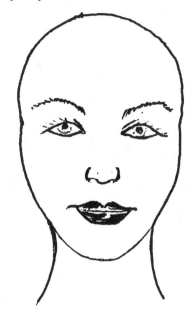

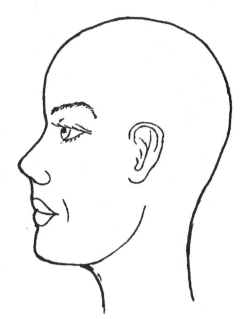

1. Draw an oval.

2. Draw features on face; if necessary, refer to the proportions on the following pages.

3. Draw a profile. Choose one of mine from below or design one of your own.

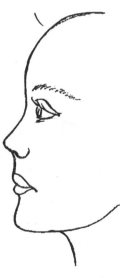

1. Turned up nose with round forehead, and large lips.

2. This is the nose I like best. average lips, square forehead.

3. Slanted forehead, pointed nose, smaller lips.

4. Younger girl, round forehead, smaller nose and lips, flatter face.

All lines of the profile are curves; no straight lines. If I establish a good profile, my face ends up good; if the profile is inadequate, it is hard to make a pretty face. As you practice drawing profiles, mix the above features, a nose from #1 with a mouth from #3, and so on. Remember that the nose is half on the face, and half protrudes beyond the upper lip line.

Carving the Female Face

21

LAYOUT OF THE FACIAL FEATURES

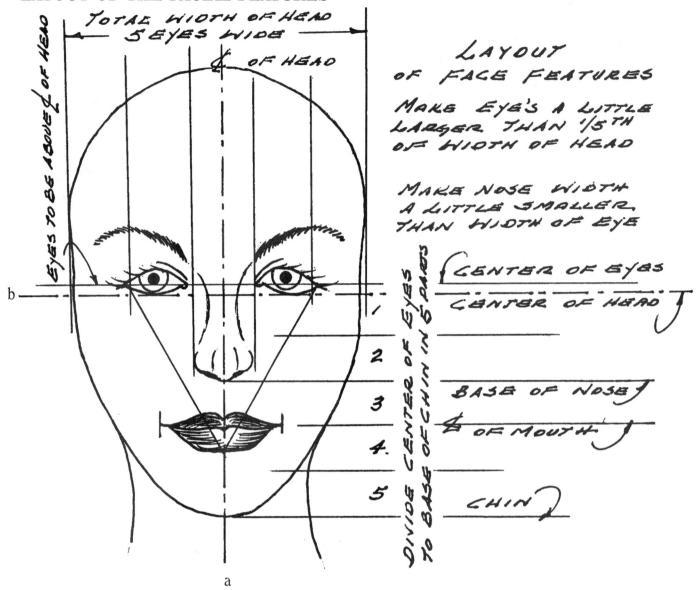

a

PUTTING IT ALL TOGETHER

1. Draw the oval for your head.
2. Vertically divide the oval into five equal parts (1–5).
3. Establish and draw in a vertical centerline of the head (a).
4. Establish and draw in a horizontal centerline of the head (b). (Note: Use wide paper and extend all horizontal lines across the wide paper so that when you draw the profile, the pattern will match front view to profile view.)
5. Draw in the eye, slightly wider than one fifth the width of the head with a center line for the eyes.
8. Divide the area from the center of the nose. The third line down will become the horizontal centerline of the mouth. (Draw an equilateral trian-gle from the outside edge of the eyes to the vertical centerline of the face to establish the bottom of the lower lip.
10. Draw in the lips, two eyes wide.
11. Draw in the nose, a little less than one eye wide. Establish the brow line, ascending from the inside one fifth line almost to the next one fifth line out, and then descend slightly to approximately two thirds the next one fifth. Study and refer to the drawing above. Notice that the neck flows from the lower cheek area toward shoulder; it does not come straight down. All of the features are curved.

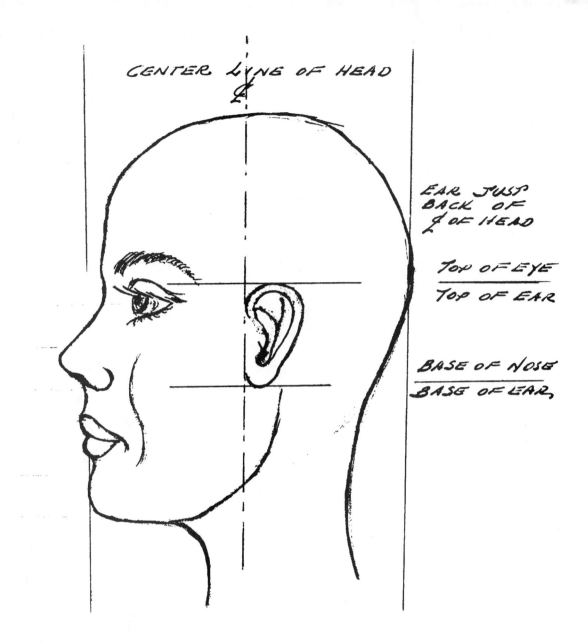

CENTER LINE OF HEAD

EAR JUST
BACK OF
₵ OF HEAD

TOP OF EYE
TOP OF EAR

BASE OF NOSE
BASE OF EAR

Draw the profile using the extended horizontal lines from the frontal view of the face for placement of the eye, nose, mouth and chin. Establish a vertical centerline through the head. The ear falls just behind that vertical line and from the top of the upper eyelid to the base of the nose. Note that the eye is an oval shape and recedes into a socket in the skull. Do not draw the eye too close to the bridge of the nose. The brow line sweeps from forward of the eye to back beyond the eye. The jaw line sweeps up behind the ear. You may wish to refer to the previous section on drawing the ear before drawing it on your full headpiece.

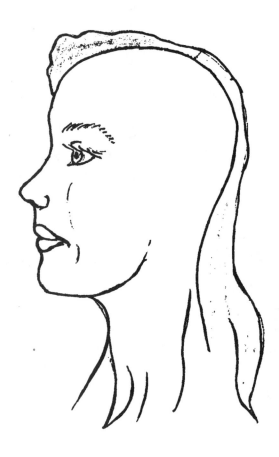

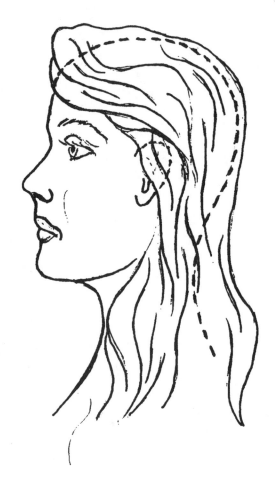

Draw the hair onto your oval and profile following the guidelines on this page. Remember that if you decide to use long hair, some of it will fall forward of the shoulder and some toward the back. It may or may not cover the ear, depending on your personal preference. The hair I have drawn partially covers the ear. Note in the profile view that it fluffs up at the front and lays closer to the skull toward the back. Drawing the hair will be similar to carving it; you should remember that hair should not look raked or manufactured. The locks should flow together in shallow curves.

Chapter Four

Building a Story Block

I recommend that you practice each of the features of the face on practice "story blocks" made up of blocks of wood approximately 2 in. by 2 in. by 14 in. (Width may vary according to your desired finished piece and length may vary according to your supply of wood.) You should carve as many copies of each feature as you need to make you feel comfortable with the wood and the feature. The 2 in. by 2 in. story block will prepare you for features up to a 4 inch face.

The corners of your story blocks should be rounded to approximately 1/2 in. to 3/4 in. from the corner in each direction. If you sand these pieces, be certain to remove all grit before beginning to carve so that you will not dull your tools. You can accomplish this by scrubbing with a stiff brush, lifting the residue with a tack cloth, or by blowing a strong air stream from a compressor.

I encourage you to take this series of practice steps quite seriously; after all, I want you to succeed and be happy with your finished product. Completing a story block will give you a guide for practicing features and completing your final project.

After preparing your practice story blocks and sharpening your tools, begin practicing the eyes. I spaced the steps on my story block approximately 1/2 in. apart.

STORY BLOCK EYES

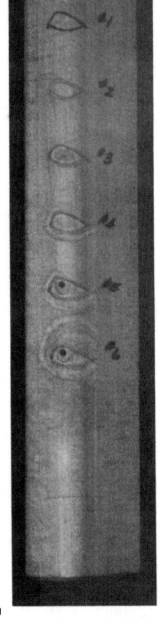

1. With a pencil, draw the outline of an eye on the story block. Draw three vertical lines the complete length of block to indicate the outer edges and the centerline of the eye.

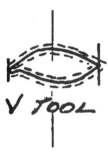

2. After you have drawn your eye, incise the lines with a small V tool along the pencil lines.

3. Next, take your knife. Holding the blade at a right angle to the wood, insert the tip of the knife in the corner of the eye. Run the knife along the lines incised by the V tool. Be careful to get this line cut to the proper depth. It should be a little deeper in the corners than at the center of the eye. Too much depth will leave you with "bugged" eyes; not enough will leave you with flat eyes.

With the knife, chip out the corners of the eye. As you can see, the eye is beginning to take on a more rounded appearance. The knife can now be used to remove a small amount from the center of the eye so that the eyeball is relieved just slightly from the lid. Remove only enough wood to cast a small shadow.

4. Choose a gouge with the same sweep as the iris. Hold the gouge perpendicular to the eye surface and scribe a line, cutting the iris in above the lower lid and up to the upper lid. With your knife, cut a small amount of wood away from the inside of the iris so that a slight shadow will be cast to indicate the iris. Mark the pupils in the exact center of the iris with a pencil. (Remember to take into consideration the part of the iris that is hidden under the upper lid when determining the center.)

5. With a medium sweep gouge, relieve around the eyelid. The top lid should be relieved from the center toward the tear duct or nose. It should begin rather shallow and deepen as it approaches the nose. The lower lid should be approximately the same depth all the way across. It should join the upper lid at the outside corner where it meets the upper lid line.

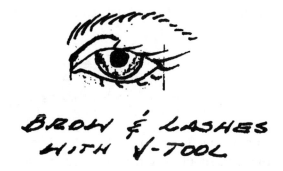

6. The next step is to incise a line for the top inside of the eyelid. Work from top to nose side with a V-tool. Incise the lashes with a V-tool. Draw in the eyebrows with a pencil and then incise them with a V-tool. Caution: Too many lashes will cheapen your results.

STORY BLOCK MOUTH

The lips are perhaps the second most important feature in determining the expression and age of a person. The same holds true for carving a face. Lips may be the essence of a female's personality. Choose the shape of lips you want your carving to have, and let's practice!

Begin by determining the width of the mouth. Normally the mouth is approximately the width of two eyes. In females, it often enhances the appearance if the eyes and mouth are a bit wider than standard. However, be careful not to overdo it.

Study mouths of the people you know. Figure out what makes the female mouth different from the male; and what makes one mouth look young and sensuous and another older and perhaps less appealing. Practice, practice! Use sharp tools! Practice with your pencil as well as with your tools.

Draw a horizontal line the width of the mouth across your next practice stick. Draw three vertical lines, two at the outside edges and one in the center.

1. Working from the center to the outside line, draw a very shallow "Cupid's bow" shape. This will be the point at which the top lip and the bottom lip meet. Pencil in the outline of the lips at this time.

2. With a V-tool, incise a shallow groove along the line where the lips meet. Follow this groove with your knife perpendicular (at right angles) to the wood. The cut should be deeper toward the center than at the outside edges.

3. With a knife, make four cuts, approximately 45 degrees, to shape the upper lip. Your cuts should begin with one cut on each side of the center of the lip, followed by a cut on each side to the outside corners.

4. To form the lower lip, make three cuts, beginning with the center and followed by each side. These cuts should also be approximately 45 degrees so that the lips are approximately at right angles.

Carving the Female Face

GOUGE UPPER

5. With a shallow gouge, relieve around the upper lip, reforming the bow that defines the top of the upper lip. Adjusting the line as you go so that the two sides are the same shape.

GOUGE LOWER

6. Using the same shallow gouge, start at the outside of the lower lip and cut down approximately 45 degrees toward the chin on both sides. Then make a deeper cut under the lower lip from one side to the other, refining the shape.

HOLLOW

CORNER
DEPRESSON
REFINE WITH
KNIFE

7. With the knife at right angles to the wood, incise a short line from the outside edge of the upper lip and on an angle in toward the chin. By cutting from the inside toward this line with a shallow stroke, you can now form a slight shadow at the corners of the mouth. With a shallow medium gouge, cut in the hollow from the center of the upper lip to the nose.

STORY BLOCK NOSE

The first step in carving a nose is obviously choosing which nose you want to carve. Understanding the structure, or anatomy, of the nose may help you grasp how the nose is formed and how it blends in to the rest of the face.

The nose is made up of cartilage, bone and a small amount of tissue.

It may help to recall the structure of the bone in the nose. It blends into the rest of the face by virtue of connecting bone, tissue and skin leading to the cheeks and to the mouth via the filtrum or hollow. It blends back into the skull bone between the eyes and the bridge of the nose.

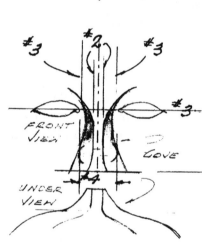

1. Beginning on a non-rounded corner of a practice stick, draw a nose on both sides of the block. Be sure they match. Use a template if you need to. Cut the profile above and below the nose.

2. After the profile material is removed, draw a centerline directly down the center of the nose. Next, draw lines approximately $1/8$ in. on each side of the centerline. These lines are not to be removed; the profile will not change from this point on.

3. Draw two vertical lines, slightly less than one eye width, to indicate the outside of nostrils. Draw a line horizontally across the bridge of the nose to indicate the eye line.

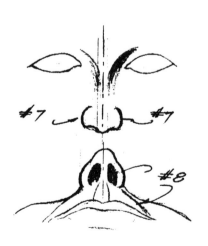

4. Draw a line on each side of the nose from the place on a vertical line where the outside of the nostril is at its widest to the spot where the $1/8$ in. outside line intersects the line indicating the eye level or the lowest place on the bridge of the nose. This will be in the shape of a cone. Study your clay model, people's noses and your practice stick lines to make certain that you have established your lines to your own satisfaction.

5. With a knife, cut the exposed part of the nostril back from the center to the side of the nostril at an angle; do not cut the inside of the three centerlines.

Carving the Female Face

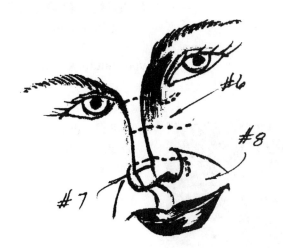

6. With a medium sweep gouge, use very shallow cuts to remove material from outside the cone line on nose. Follow the line of the cone, veering in toward the eye in the bridge area. Remember that the nose should blend into the face and the cheekbone gently; therefore, remove only a small amount of the wood in this area until you achieve the desired depth.

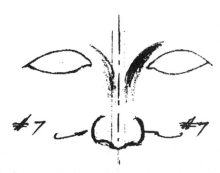

7. Choose a gouge that matches the shape of the outside of the nostril. Cut directly from the outside of the nostril and go straight into the wood perpendicular to the nose.

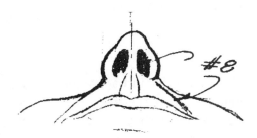

8. Using the same shallow gouge, relieve a shallow area from the outside of the mouth in the mid/lower cheek area in toward the nostril, undercutting the nostril only slightly. (Do not cut too deep, or too far into the nose, thus cutting into the nostril.) This will be the cut that begins to form the cone for the mouth. With a deep gouge, cut the inside of the nostril. Don't cut away the three centerlines.

9. Make adjustments where necessary. Remember to take very shallow cuts, removing only a small amount of wood at a time. You can always take a little more off; putting it back can be a problem.

STORY BLOCK EARS

Ears, although frequently covered by hair or a hat, are a part of the anatomy of the face and head. I am including them here so that the information will be available to you should you decide to use it.

1. Begin by drawing the top-heavy C of the ear on your story block. With a small, deep gouge, follow the outline of the top-heavy C.

2. Next, draw in the inside C. With a small, shallow gouge, follow that line from bottom to the top (or crest) from each side. Change to a small, deep gouge and finish the cut by gradually going deeper from the backside to the inside, upper face-side area of the ear. Slightly undercut the helix at the very top. Using a shallow gouge, remove the wood in the area between the lines of the inside C.

3. Draw in the lazy Y and the running U. With a shallow gouge, remove the wood in the fork of the Y. Still using the shallow gouge, cut around the tragus with a perpendicular cut to the wood. With a deeper gouge, make the cut perpendicular to the wood just below the tragus. Again, with the shallow gouge, make a diagonal cut to chip out the other two cuts, relieving the area slightly below the tragus.

4. Relieve the bottom inside of the big C, or helix, just above the tragus with a shallow gouge. Refine the fork of the area between the forks of the Y. In the lobe of the ear, you may want to make a shallow depression to give the ear a little more character.

5. Undercut around the outside of the ear with a knife or a very small gouge, followed by a shallow gouge coming in toward the ear. Finish by refining your cuts, if necessary, with a knife and sandpaper.

Carving the Female Face

Chapter Five

Model

In the next section of this book, I present an exercise in putting all of the features together. I feel that making a model of the face can be of great help to you in your carving efforts, not only in the carving of your final piece, but also for the sake of carving other faces. You can use this model for getting perspective in drawing, for carving relief faces, and for study.

It is important that you practice each feature on story-block pieces of wood before you put that feature on the model. Remember that your pencil is one of your friendliest tools; you can erase or remove the marks with sandpaper.

If you have difficulty matching the eyes, try cutting out a template and tracing the eyes. You can flip the templates for an exact replica on the opposite side. The same holds true of the mouth, only it may be easier to make a template of the whole mouth.

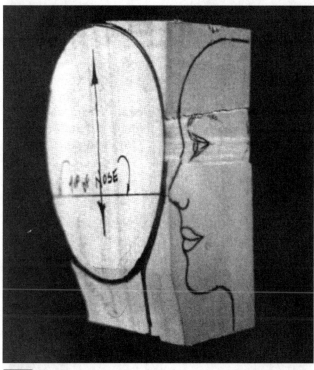

1 Begin with a firm basswood block measuring 2 in. by 4 in. by 6 in. with the grain running the 6-in length. Draw a profile on each side of the block, making sure that the features match. Work from a template or pattern. The tip of the nose is a good reference point for aligning the two sides of the block. You might want to draw horizontal lines across the block at the tip of the nose, the eye line, and the center of the lips to make certain that the two sides of the block match perfectly.

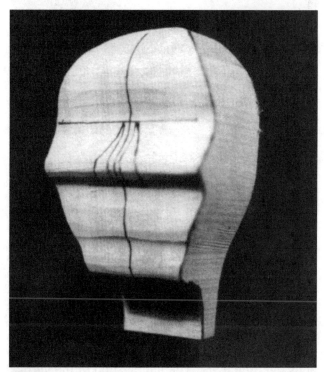

2 Secure the block in a vice and using shallow and deep gouges from 12 mm 1/2 in. to 18 mm 1 in., cut directly across the block from guideline to guideline to form as perfect a profile as possible. Using a very dark pencil or a felt-tipped marker, draw on the oval from the front view and cut the oval of the head on a band saw or with chisels. Draw in the vertical centerline of the head and the cone for the nose. Draw two vertical lines 1/8 in. on both sides of the centerline from the bridge to the under side of the nose. These lines will not be removed during the carving.

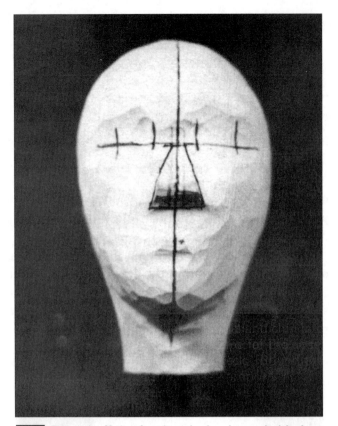

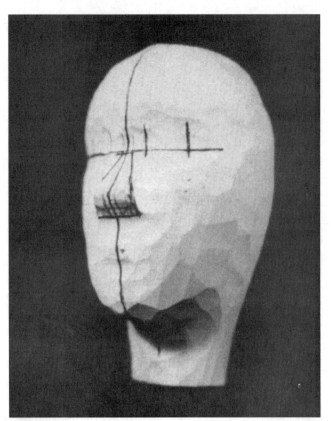

3 Round off the forehead, cheeks and chin into an oval, leaving the cone shape for the nose. Roll off under the chin into the neck. Round the neck.

4 Using a shallow gouge, begin to form shallow sockets for the eyes. Cut from outside up toward the bridge of the nose to 1/2" of the centerline. Remember, the eye is a ball, so maintain a curve up to the crest from the outside and from the crest toward the tear duct. Don't forget, females are all curves, no flat areas.

5 Referring to "Layout of the Facial Features" (page 22), draw reference lines for the features. Check all measurements, proportions and locations of features and adjust until they are to your satisfaction. It will help to draw lines across the bridge of the nose, through the eye area, at the base of the nose, and at the center of the mouth. Draw vertical lines to indicate the outer edges of the eyes and the centerline of the eye. Extend these lines up over the brow and onto the forehead so that you can redraw them after cutting away the lines over the eyes. The intersection of the vertical line and the horizontal line through the center of the eye will remain and continue to indicate the crest of the ball of the eye.

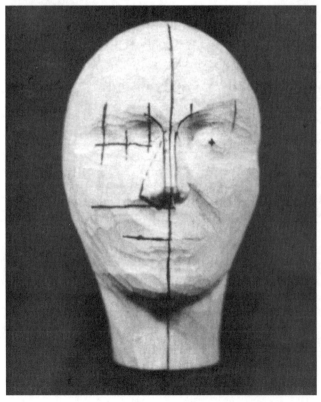

Carving the Female Face

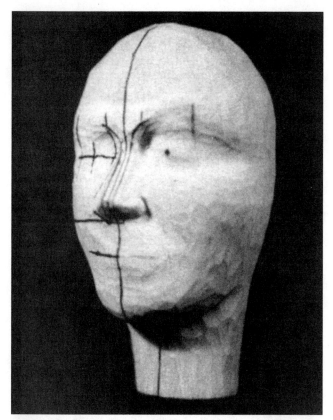 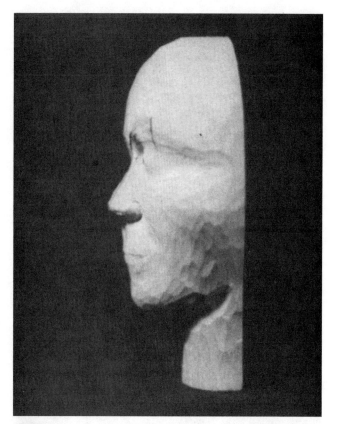

6 With a medium-sized shallow gouge, cut from the centerline of the eye toward the bridge of the nose, stopping at the tear duct eye line. With a shallow gouge, make shallow cuts from the outer triangle of the nose toward the area between the tear duct and the bridge of the nose. As you cut be sure to never remove the lines on top of the nose. Leave the top of the nose flat!

Using a deep 6mm gouge, make a cut from just below the bridge of the nose to the area between the tear duct and the bridge of the nose. With the same gouge, cut from the centerline of the eye and just above the eye to the tear duct, meeting the cut up from the nose. Be aware that there is a grain change here and that you can not make that cut all in one sweep. Again, removing small amounts of wood at a time may be preferable to one large mistake. The cut down from the top center of the eye is also beginning to define the ball of the eye.

7 With a shallow gouge, form a football shape by cutting around the top of the eye and between the eye socket and the cheek. The only lines you will have left on the eye itself will be a tiny point at the crest of the eyeball. Do not cut the eyeball off; leave the eyeball round, not flat.

With a knife, cut the exposed part of the nostril at an angle back from the line drawn by the centerline to the side of the nostril; do not cut inside the three centerlines. With a medium sweep gouge, use very shallow cuts to remove material from outside the cone line on the nose; be sure to follow the line of the cone. Remember that the nose should blend into the face and the cheekbone gently; therefore, remove only a small amount of wood in this area at a time until you achieve the desired depth.

At the intersection of the outside line of the nose and the horizontal line beneath the nose, make a perpendicular cut with a 4mm shallow gouge. Cut both sides of the nostril. With the same gouge relieve a shallow area from the outside of the mouth in the mid/lower cheek area in to the nostril. (Caution: Do not cut too deep or too far in; you may cut into the nostril.) This cut will begin to form the cone for the mouth.

Make adjustments where necessary. Remember to take very shallow cuts, removing only a small amount of wood at a time.

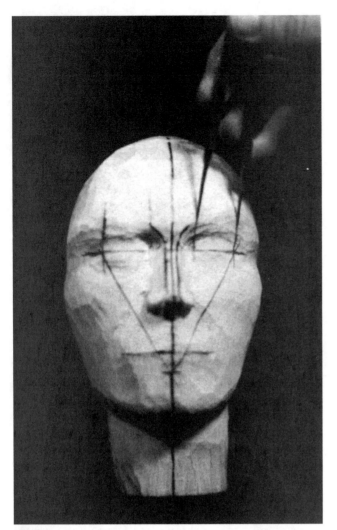

8 Using a shallow gouge, refine the feature until the surfaces are nice and round in the areas of the mouth and eyes. If you decide to use sandpaper at this point, be sure to remove all grit so that you will not dull your tools. Refer to the reference section of this book and "Layout of the Facial Features" on page 22. Use the centerline as a reference point. A triangle from outside of the eyes to just below the mouth will help you define the mouth placement more accurately, or you can check this distance with a pair of dividers.

Draw another horizontal line across the bridge of the nose to define the center of the eyes. Draw the features on, making certain that the two sides of the face match. The left eye and the right eye should match as perfectly as possible. A common error is to not align the eyes horizontally. The left side of the mouth should match the right side of the mouth. Make a template if you need to and trace the lines onto the practice block. A good mouth will help you maintain the eyes in alignment. Bring down the vertical reference lines from the forehead to define the outside limits of the eyes.

9 With a pencil, draw the outline of an eye on your block. After you have drawn your eye, incise the lines with a small V-tool. Next, take your knife, and with the blade at right angle to your wood, insert the tip in each corner and run the knife along the line incised by your V-tool. You must be careful to get this line cut to the proper depth: a little deeper in the corners than at the center of the eye. Too much depth will leave you with "bugged" eyes; not enough will leave you with flat eyes.

10 With your knife, chip out the corners of the eye. As you can see, the eye is beginning to take on a more rounded appearance. Now use a knife to remove a small amount of wood from the center of the eye so that the eyeball is relieved from the lid just <u>slightly.</u> Remove only enough wood to cast barely a shadow.

With a gouge the same sweep as you want your iris, holding it perpendicular to the eye surface, scribe a line, cutting the iris in above the lower lid and up to the upper lid. With your knife, cut a small amount of wood away from the inside of the iris so that a slight shadow will be cast, indicating the iris. Mark with a pencil and cut in the pupils in the exact center of the iris. (Remember to take into consideration the part of the iris that is hidden under the upper lid when determining the center.) Do not hide any part of the pupil under the lid. Make the pupils completely round.

With a medium sweep gouge, relieve around the eyelid. The top lid should be relieved from the center toward the tear duct or nose and should begin rather shallow and deepen as it approaches the nose. (Switch to a deeper gouge as you approach the tear duct.) The lower lid should be approximately the same depth all the way across and should meet the upper lid just under the outside corner. Note: The brow on the inner side of the eye is concave; the outer side is convex. Lashes may be incised. (Caution: too many lashes will cheapen your results.) Draw the brow hair in with a pencil and then incise it with a V-tool. To emphasize the eyes even more, carve a line above the upper lid of the eye from the center down into the tear duct, indicating the fold in the eyelid.

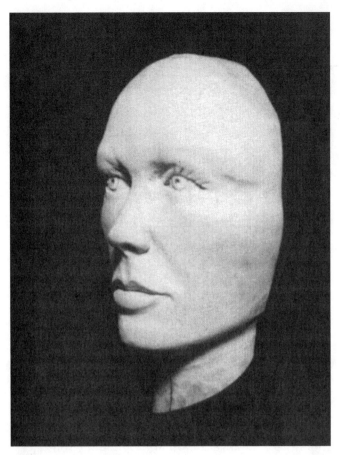

11 Draw a horizontal line the width of the mouth. Draw three vertical lines, two at the outside edges and one in the center. Working from the center to the outside line, draw a very shallow "Cupid's bow" shape. This will be the point at which the top lip and the bottom lip meet. Draw in the outline of the lips at this time. With a V-tool, incise a shallow groove along the line where the lips meet.

Follow this groove with your knife perpendicular (at right angles) to the wood. This cut should be deeper toward the center than at the outside edges. With the knife, make four cuts, on an approximately 45-degree angle from the surface, to shape the upper lip. Your cuts should begin with one cut on each side of the center of the lip followed by a cut on each side to the outside corners.

To form the lower lip, you should make three cuts, beginning with the center followed by each side. These cuts should also be approximately 45 degrees so that the lips are approximately at right angles.

With a shallow gouge, relieve around the lower lip, from the center to the edge, going slightly deeper at the corners of the mouth. You may repeat this cut at the top of the lip, adjusting slightly to match the sides of the lips.

With the knife at right angles to the wood, incise a short line from the outside edge of the upper lip and on an angle in toward the chin. By cutting from the inside toward this line with a shallow stroke, you can now form a slight shadow at the corners of the mouth. With a shallow medium gouge, cut in the hollow from the center of the upper lip to the nose. At this point, you can refine the area around the mouth and make any adjustments necessary to make the mouth match one side to the other.

Chapter Six

Final Piece

In preparing for your final piece, you can either design your own pattern, lining up the features on the face and matching the profile and the head size and adding adornments such as hair, a hat, flowers or you may choose any of the patterns in this book. You might wish to enlarge one by reproducing it on a copy machine. Be sure to make the profile features and the front features match.

Next, select a firm basswood block large enough for your pattern, with the grain running the length. Draw a profile on each side of the block with a felt-tipped pen, making sure that the features match.

1 Draw the pattern on the front of the block; this will serve the purpose of assuring that your pattern and wood will be compatible. Work from a template or pattern. I used the pattern on pages 46 and 47. Draw horizontal lines across the block at the tip of the nose, the eye line, and the center of the lips to make certain that the two sides of the block match perfectly.

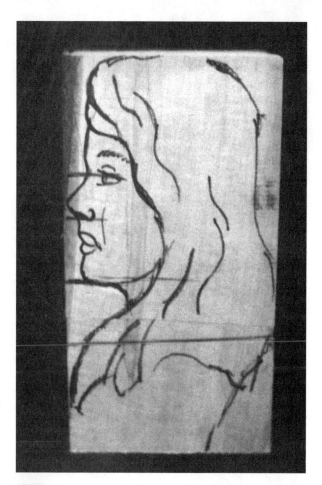

2 Draw the profile view on each side of the block. The tip of the nose is a good reference point for aligning the pattern on the block.

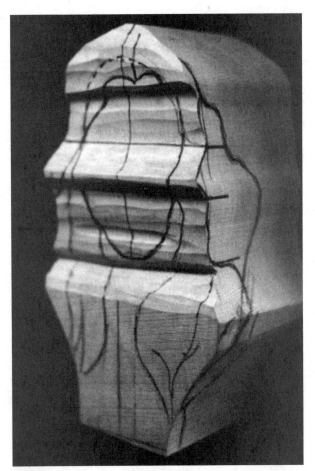

3 Secure the block in a vise. Using shallow and deep gouges of the appropriate size for your pattern, cut directly across the block from guideline to guideline to form as perfect a profile as possible. Using a very dark pencil or a felt-tipped marker, draw on the front view. Cut the front view of the head with a band saw or with chisels.

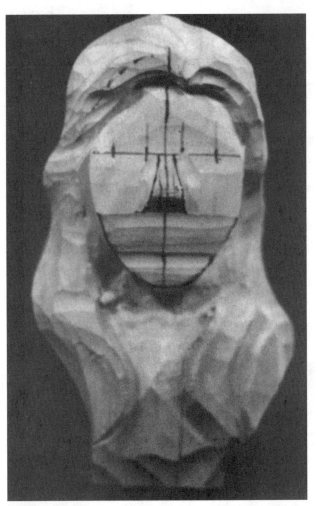

4 Draw in the vertical centerline of the head and the cone for the nose. With a pencil, draw two vertical lines 1/8 in. on both sides of the centerline from the bridge to the under side of the nose. These lines will not be removed during the carving.

Carving the Female Face

5 Round off the forehead, cheeks and chin into an oval, leaving the cone shape for the nose. Roll off under the chin into the neck. Round the neck, leaving the hairline and clothing as needed. You can take a V-tool or a deep gouge to begin an outline around the hairline. The thing to remember is that the forehead must be rounded, not flat. You must have enough room to round the cheek, and the oval of the face must emerge as you cut the hairline back. The hairline will usually protrude beyond the forehead.

Using a shallow gouge, begin to form the shallow sockets for the eyes. Cut from the vertical centerline of the eye toward the bridge of the nose to 1/2" of the vertical centerline of the face. Then cut from the vertical centerline of the eye into the temple area. Remember: the eye is a ball, so maintain a curve up to the crest from the outside and from the crest toward the tear duct. Don't forget to retain the feminine curves all the way through your piece.

Referring to "Layout of the Facial Features" on page 22, draw reference lines for the features. Check all measurements, proportions and locations of features and adjust them until they are to your satisfaction. It will help to draw lines across the bridge of the nose, through the eye area, at the base of the nose, and at the center of the mouth

Draw vertical lines to indicate the outer edges of the eyes and the centerline of the eye. Extend these lines up over the brow and onto the forehead so that you can redraw them after cutting away the lines over the eyes. The intersection of the vertical line and the horizontal line through the center of the eye will remain and continue to indicate the crest of the ball of the eye.

6 With a medium-sized shallow gouge, cut from the centerline of the eye toward the bridge of the nose, stopping at the tear duct eye line. With a shallow gouge, make shallow cuts from the outer triangle of the nose toward the area between the tear duct and the bridge of the nose, never removing the lines on top of the nose. Leave the top of the nose flat!

Using a deep 6-mm gouge, make a cut from just below the bridge of the nose to the area between the tear duct and the bridge of the nose. With the same gouge cut from the centerline of the eye and just above the eye to the tear duct, meeting the cut up from the nose. Be aware that there is a grain change here and that you cannot make that cut all in one sweep. Again, removing small amounts of wood at a time may be preferable to making one large mistake. The cut down from the top center of the eye is also beginning to define the ball of the eye.

With a shallow gouge, form a football shape by cutting around the top of the eye and between the eye socket and the cheek. The only line you will have left on the eye itself will be a tiny point at the crest of the eyeball. Do not cut the eyeball off; leave the eyeball round, not flat.

With a knife, cut the exposed part of the nostril at an angle back from the line drawn by the centerline to the side of the nostril; do not cut inside the three centerlines. With a medium sweep gouge, use very shallow cuts to remove material from outside the cone line on the nose; be sure to follow the line of the cone. Remember that the nose should blend into the face and the cheekbone gently; therefore, remove only a small amount of wood in this area at a time until you achieve the desired depth.

At the intersection of the outside line of the nose and the horizontal line beneath the nose, make a perpendicular cut with a 4-mm shallow gouge. Cut both sides of the nostril. With the same gouge relieve a shallow area from the outside of the mouth in the mid/lower cheek area in to the nostril. (Caution: Do not cut too deep or too far in; you may cut into the nostril.) This cut will begin to form the cone for the mouth.

7 Make adjustments where necessary. Remember to take very shallow cuts, removing only a small amount of wood at a time.

Using a shallow gouge, refine the features until the surfaces are nice and round in the areas of the mouth and eyes. If you decide to use sandpaper at this point, be sure to remove all grit so that you will not dull your tools. Refer to drawing section of this book, and lay out the features. Using the centerline as a reference point. A triangle from outside the eyes to just below the mouth will help you in defining the mouth placement more accurately, or you can check this distance with a pair of dividers. I suggest that you use a pencil, not ink for this part of the layout. Ink tends to be more difficult to remove and must be cut away, as opposed to pencil, which may be sanded away.

Draw another horizontal line across the bridge of the nose to define the center of the eyes. Bring down the vertical reference lines from the forehead to define the outside limits of the eyes. Draw the features on, making certain that the two sides of the face match; the left eye and the right eye should match as perfectly as possible. A common error is to not align the eyes horizontally. The left side of the mouth should match the right side of the mouth. Make a template if you need to and trace the lines onto the piece. This will help you to maintain your eyes in alignment.

Although we have divided this section into facial feature parts, it is important to remember that no one part of the face should be completed before the other parts. Work a little on each area at a time until the whole emerges complete and to your satisfaction. As you remove the lines with your gouges, replace the lines you will need for future reference.

Carving the Female Face

EYES

The story block that you built from prior instructions in this book will act as an aid to completing your final piece. Practicing each feature on a rounded story block before applying your tools to your final piece will give you more desirable results.

With a pencil, draw the outline of an eye on your block. After you have drawn your eye, incise the lines with a small v-tool, along your pencil lines. Next, take your knife, and with the blade at a right angle to your wood insert the tip in each corner and run the knife along the line incised by your v-tool. You must be careful to get this line cut to the proper depth, a little deeper in the corners than at the center of the eye. Too much depth will leave you with "bugged" eyes, and not enough will leave you with flat eyes.

With your knife, chip out the corners of the eye. As you can see, your eye is beginning to take on a more rounded appearance. Your knife can now be used to remove a small amount from the center of the eye so that the eyeball is relieved from the lid just <u>slightly.</u> Barely enough to cast a shadow is needed here.

With a gouge the same sweep as you want your iris, holding it perpendicular to the eye surface, scribe a line, cutting the iris in above the lower lid and up to the upper lid. With your knife, cut a small amount of wood away from the inside of the iris so that a slight shadow will be cast, indicating the iris. (Remember to take into consideration the part of the iris that is hidden under the upper lid when determining the center.) Do not hide any part of the pupil under the lid. Make the pupils completely round.

With a medium sweep gouge, relieve around the eyelid. The top lid should be relieved from the center toward the tear duct of nose and should begin rather shallow and deepen as it approaches the nose. (Switch to a deeper gouge as you approach the tear duct.) The lower lid should be

approximately the same depth all the way across and should meet the upper lid just under the outside corner. Note: The brow on the inner side of the eye is concave, the outer side is convex.

Lashes may be incised (Caution: Too many lashes will cheapen your results.) Draw the brow hair in with pencil and then incise with a v-tool; incise a line above the upper lid of the eye from the center down into the tear duct indicating the fold in the eyelid to emphasize the eyes even more.

MOUTH

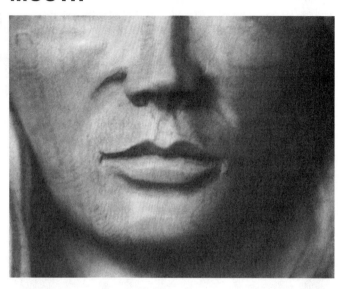

Draw a horizontal line the width of the mouth. Draw three vertical lines, two at the outside edges and one in the center. Working from the center to the outside line, draw a very shallow "Cupid's Bow" shape. This will be the point at which the top lip and the bottom lip meet. Draw in the outline of the lips at this time. With a v-tool, incise a shallow groove along the line you drew where the lips meet.

Follow this groove with your knife perpendicular (at right angles) to the wood. It should be deeper toward the center than at the outside edges. With your knife, make four cuts, on approximately 45-degree angle from the surface, to shape the upper lip. Your cuts should begin with one on each side of the center of the lip followed by a cut on each side to the outside corners.

To form the lower lip, you should make three cuts, beginning with the center followed by each side. These cuts should also be approximately 45 degrees so that the lips are approximately at right angles.

With a shallow gouge, relieve around lower lip, from center to edge, going slightly deeper at the corners of the mouth. You may repeat this at the top of the lip and adjusting slightly to match the sides of the lips.

With your knife at right angles to the wood,

incise a short line from the outside edge of the upper lip and on an angle in toward the chin. By cutting from the inside toward this line with a shallow stroke, you can now form a slight shadow at the corners of the mouth. With a shallow medium gouge, cut in the hollow from the center of the upper lip to the nose.

At this point, you can refine around the mouth and make any adjustments necessary to make the mouth match one side to the other. The lips can be separated slightly with a knife to cast more of a shadow and further define the opening between them. An emery board will help smooth the lips and round the bottom lip up into the division between the two lips. When you sand below the lower lip, be careful not to destroy the profile drop toward the chin; it is more severe than the upper portion. I use sandpaper wrapped around a dowel in the center portion. The outer edges should blend into the face more gently. The results will be a deep shadow cast under the center of the mouth and a slight shadow under the outside corners of the upper lip.

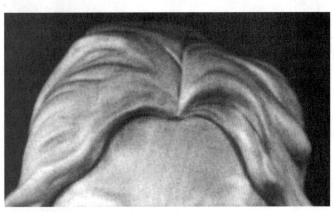

HAIR

The hair can be worked on either during the facial work or later. I find that working on the hair is sometimes a relief from the tedious work of the face. When you find yourself making mistakes or feeling tired, you might try moving to the hair for a while.

To form natural-looking hair, begin by drawing on some flowing lines. Use shallow "S" lines of different lengths along side each other in a staggered fashion from top to bottom. The lines should be appropriately spaced; do not get them too close together or too even. Hair is not uniform and should not look "raked." Study photos and my patterns. (The darker areas are where the gouge will go the deepest.) Notice too that occasionally the hair that grows from the back of the head will come over the shoulder, and the hair from the front will flow back behind it.) Next, take a large, deep sweep gouge and follow the lines. Follow this furrow with

smaller and smaller gouges until the hair looks natural and falls in locks to frame the face. I find it preferable, where possible, to follow the contour from top to bottom, the same direction hair naturally grows. The hair should be finished by sanding inside each of the depressions formed by the gouges

I wrap the sandpaper around different sizes of objects to reach all of the creases. A pencil eraser or chopsticks that have been rounded off on one end make good tools for this task. The chopsticks can also be used to burnish some of the grooves with the sandpaper wrapping.

Spending a great deal of time on the hair, which is the frame of the face, may mean the difference between a good piece and a terrific work of art.

FINISHING TOUCHES

In a straight-ahead stance, a female will have slightly raised areas in the neck indicating the ligaments. A slight indentation lies between the ligaments. When the head is turned, even slightly, adjust the neck cords appropriately. Study this feature in women. If exposed, the clavical bones will show slightly.

I have found that the v-tool is the greatest enemy of the novice carver when carving the face. Shallow gouges are more effective, and leave a prettier result except in the areas specifically designated to deeper gouges or to the v-tool.

It is a good idea to do all of your smoothing, sanding and cleaning up prior to adjusting and putting the finishing touches on the face. By viewing the face from all angles, you can determine if one eye is a little high or if the mouth needs to be moved slightly up or down. View the face from under, over, full profile from both sides, three-quarter view and every other way you can turn her in order to check for balance and symmetry.

I hope that this method has assisted you in reaching your goal of carving a pretty face. The close-up pictures of eyes, mouth, and nose that follow will help you to understand the cuts in the eyes and the cuts at the corner of the mouth. You can also see how the nose blends into the face. The nose seems to be the most difficult feature to explain in words, and as you will note, I took an extra amount of time and effort with the nose in the story block section of this book. There is a tendency among novices to carve the nose in such a manner as to make it look as though it had been stuck on the face in afterthought.

Patterns

© Wally Lueth

© Wally Lueth

Carmelita

© Wally Lueth

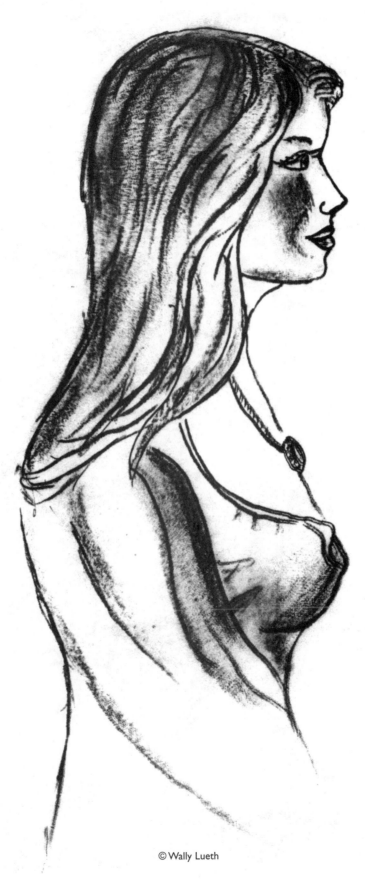

Miss Roaring Twenties

© Wally Lueth

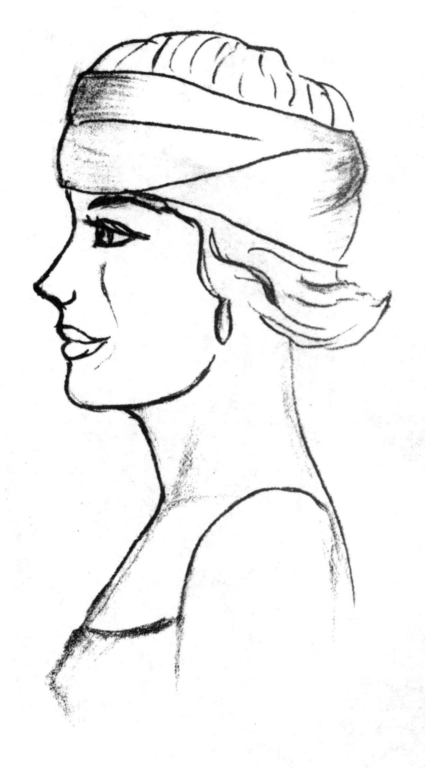

© Wally Lueth

Missy

© Wally Lueth

© Wally Lueth

Queen of Hearts

© Wally Lueth

© Wally Lueth

Mary Lou

© Wally Lueth

© Wally Lueth

© Wally Lueth

Carving the Female Face

© Wally Lueth

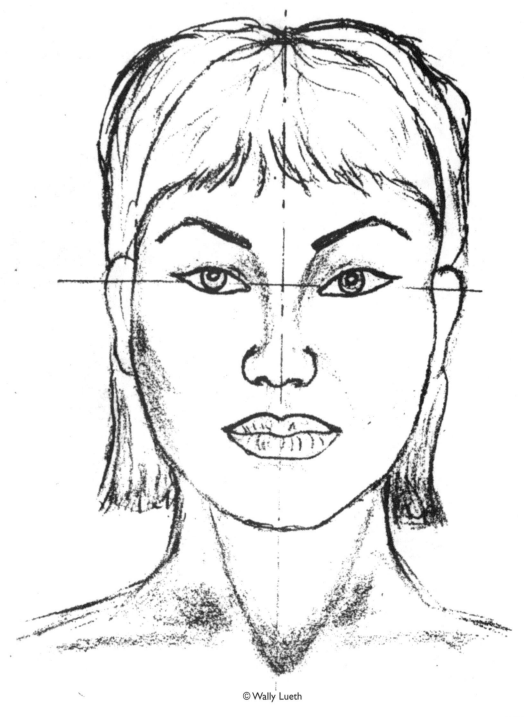

© Wally Lueth

ORIENTAL

Carving the Female Face

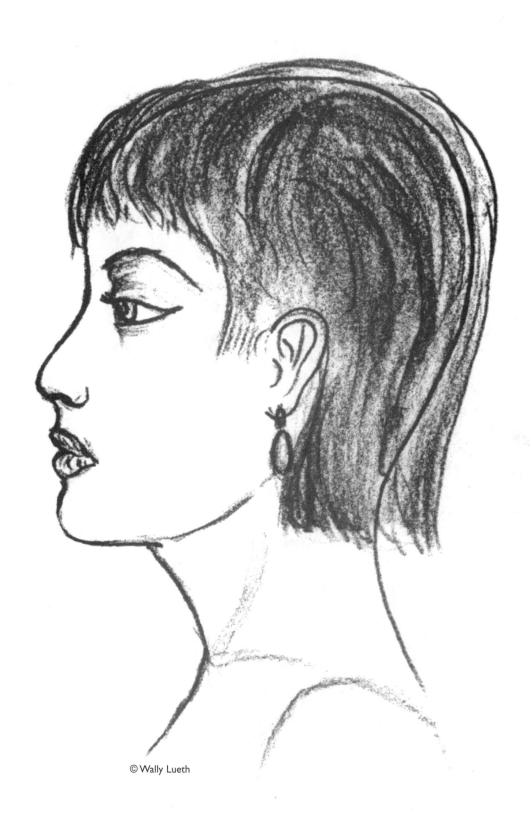

© Wally Lueth

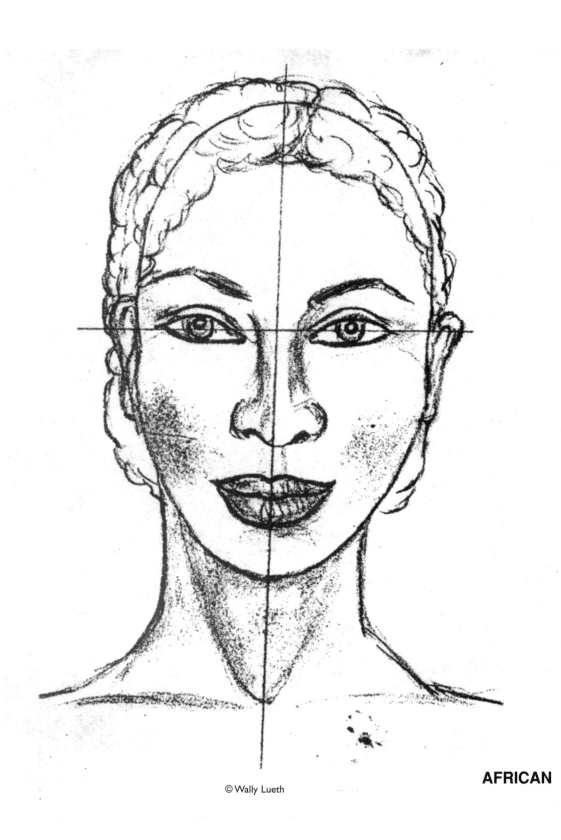

AFRICAN

© Wally Lueth

© Wally Lueth

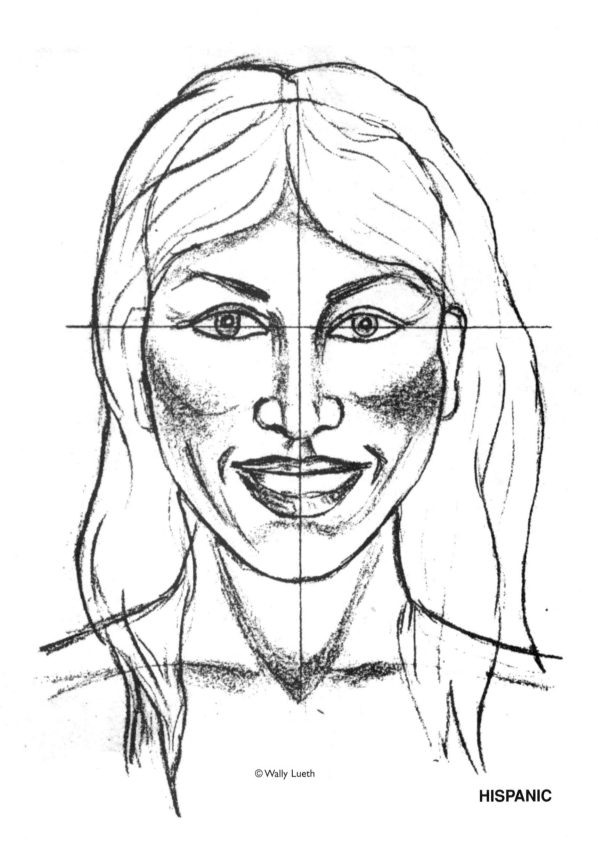

© Wally Lueth

HISPANIC

© Wally Lueth

© Wally Lueth

© Wally Lueth

© Wally Lueth

© Wally Lueth

© Wally Lueth

© Wally Lueth